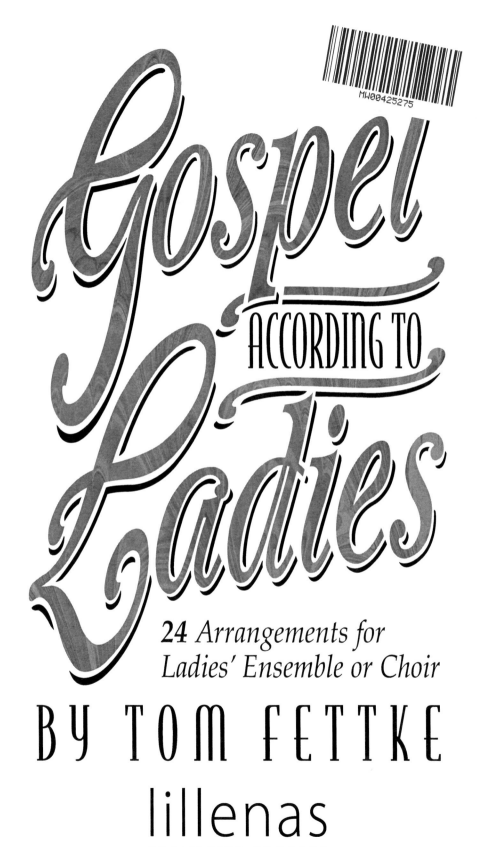

Gospel According to Ladies

24 *Arrangements for Ladies' Ensemble or Choir*

BY TOM FETTKE

lillenas
PUBLISHING COMPANY

CONTENTS

Coming Down

(S. S. A.)

W. H.

WES HOMN
Arr. by Tom Fe

Hallelujah! Praise the Lamb
(S. S. A.)

P. T., D. T. and G. McS.

PAM THUM, DAWN THOM
and GARY McSPADD
Arr. by Mosie Li
S.S.A. arr. by Tom Fe

sac - ri - fice, re - stor-ing to Him-self His own a - gain.

So the Lamb, God's on - ly Son, was free - ly of - fered,____

All, un

tone- ment for our sin for - ev - er made. He,

in - no - cent and ho - ly, still God____ and God on - ly coul

Holy Lamb of God

[S. S. A. (A.)]
A cappella

MOSIE LISTER
Arr. by Tom Fettke

There's Still Power in the Blood

(S. S. A.)

K. T.

KIRK TALL
Arr. by Tom Fe

say that in this mod - ern day___ love is all you need.___ I've
sins were washed a - way___when I stepped in the cleans - ing flood.___

C   A7/C#   Dm   C/E   F

CD: 9   1st time
CD: 10   2nd time

nev - er seen a love___ more tried___ and test - ed   Than the
When I'm need - ing vic - t'ry o - ver Sa - tan,   I jus

A   A/C#   Dsus   Dm   C/D   Dm7

1

f Div.

love___ that came stream - ing down__ the cross of Cal - va - ry.___ There's still
stand my ground,___ look at Him___ and

Gsus   G   Csus   C   C7

2

Div.

I claim the blood!   There's still

Csus   C   Dsus   D

gliss.

pow - er in the blood___ of the Lamb.___

35 "I Know a Fount" (Oliver Cooke)
Stay strong

Bur - dens are lift - ed, blind eyes made to see; There's a

39 **CD: 11**

Stronger
Unison

won - der-work-ing pow'r in the blood of Cal - va - ry. There's still

43

pow - er in the blood___ of Je - sus, Hope in a trou-bled dy-i

The Way of the Cross Led Me Home

(S. S. A.)

M. L.

MOSIE LIST

Arr. by Randy Smith and Tom Fe
S. S. A. arr. by Tom Fe

(33)

home."

"Child, come home." And thro'-out end-less a - ges I'

(37)

sing His praise; For the way of the cross, th

(41)

old rug-ged cross, The__ way of the cross led m

CD: 13

home. These__

Bright and Morning Star

(S. S. A.)

Arr. by Tom Fettke

*"The Lily of the Valley" (Charles Fry - William Hays)

found a friend in Je-sus; He's ev-'ry-thing to me. He's the fair-est of ten thou-sand to my

soul. The___ Lil-y of the Val-ley, in Him a-lone I see All

need to cleanse and make me ful-ly whole. In

sor-row He's my com-fort; in trou-ble He's my stay. He___

tells me ev-'ry care on Him to roll. He's the

*"It's Just Like His Great Love" (Edna Worrell - Clarence Strouse)

friend I have, called Je - sus,_____ Whose love is strong and

true_____ And nev - er fails, how - e'er 'tis tried— No

mat - ter what I do._____ I've sinned a - gainst this

love of His; But when I knelt to pray, Con

fess - ing all my guilt to Him, The

sin - clouds rolled a - way. It's

just like Je - sus to roll the clouds a- way. It's just like Je - sus to

keep me day by day. It's just like Je - sus all a- long the way. It's

CD: 19

Alto Solo (or se

just like His great love._____ O

I could sing for - ev - er Of Je - sus' love di

vine– Of all His care and ten - der - ness F

cresc.

this poor life of mine. His

Sop. II and a

just like Je - sus to roll the clouds a-way. It's just like Je - sus

keep me day by day. It's just like Je - sus all a-long the way. It

CD: 21

just like His great love. It's

just like Je - sus to roll the clouds a-way. It's just like Je - sus

keep me day by day. It's just like Je - sus all a- long the way.

It's just like His great

love, re - deem - ing love.

For What Earthly Reason
(S. S. A.)

D. R.

DOTTIE RAM
Arr. by Tom Fe

"what earth - ly rea - son" was me.

fair - est of an - gels were not sum - moned from the throne up in th

The

112
y,_____ He was the sac - ri -

Fm/Eb Bb/D Cm7 Bb7 Bb13 Bb9 Ab/Eb

116
fice._____ I was the tak -

Eb Db/Eb Eb Fm7 Eb/G Ab

120
er;_____ He was the giv -

Cm7/G Fm7 Ab/Bb Bb7 Ab/Bb Ab/Eb

decresc.

124
er,_____ Dy - ing while I_____ go

Eb Bbm6/Db C7 C+ C7 F9sus Fm

decresc.

I've Never Been This Homesick Before

(S. S. A.)

DOTTIE RAMBO
Arr. by Joseph Linn
S. S. A. arr. by Tom Fettke

Up tempo country shuffle ♩ = ca. 136

There's a light in the win-dow; the ta-ble's spread in splen-dor. Some-one's stand-ing by the o-pen door.

home - sick be - fore. See the bright___

fore. See the bright___ light shine;

It's just a-bout___ home - time.___ I can

see my Fa-ther stand - ing___ at the door.

Coming Again

[S. S. A. (A.)]
A cappella

MOSIE LISTER
Arr. by Tom Fettke

L.

p Unison

Je - sus is com - ing; Je - sus is com - ing;

Je - sus is com - ing, He's com - ing a - gain.

mp Div.

In clouds of glo - ry, In clouds of glo - ry,

In clouds of glo - ry He's com - ing a - gain, a - gain.

mf

We'll rise to meet Him, Rise up to meet Him;

Opt. low alto

We'll rise to meet Him. He's com - ing a - gain, a - gain.

What a Day That Will Be

(S. S. A.)

JIM HILL
Arr. by Tom Fettke and Randy Smith
S.S.A. arr. by Tom Fettke

With anticipation ♩. = ca. 67

CD: 31

f

Unison *mf*

mf

There is

⑦

com - ing a day when no heart - aches shall

(35)

Land, What a day, glo-ri-ous day that w[ill]

CD: 32

be!

decresc.

Alto solo (freely)
mp

(41)

There'll be no sor-row there, no mo[re]

mp

(45)

bur - dens to bear, No more sick-ness, n[o]

pain, no more part - ing o - ver there. And for-

ev - er I will be with the One_____ who died for

Sopranos (or all)

Oo_____

me._____ What a day, glo-ri-ous

Oo_____

CD: 33

day   that will be!

cresc.

mf

What a day that w

mf

60

be   when my Je - sus I shall see,   And

look____ up-on His face– the One who saved____ me by His

cresc.

grace. When He takes____ me by the hand____ and leads me

f

through____ the Prom-ised Land, What a day, glo-ri-ous

day that will be!____ What a

cresc.

ff

CD: 34

62

day that will be when my Je - sus I sh[all]

see, And I look____ up-on His face– the One wh[o]

saved____ me by His grace, by His grace. When He

takes____ me by the hand and leads me through____ the Prom-ise[d]

Good Old Gospel Singing

(S. S. A.)

with optional congregational participation on

When We All Get to Heaven
Leaning on the Everlasting Arms
Since Jesus Came Into My Heart

Arr. by Tom Fet

*"Good Old Gospel Singing" (Mosie Lister)

I love that good old gos- pel sing-in

Hap - py gos-pel sing- ing, Ring - ing out so loud and clear;

23 *"When We All Get to Heaven" (Hewitt - Wilson)

58

Lean - ing, lean - ing, Safe and se - cure from all a - larms;

62

Lean - ing, lean - ing, Lean - ing on the ev - er -

CD: 39

last - ing arms! I love that

69

good old gos-pel sing-ing, Hap - py gos-pel sing - ing, Ring - ing out so loud and

Satisfied

(S. S. A.)

TRADITIONAL

TRADITIONA[L]
Arr. by Tom Fett[]

* If alto part is too low, this arrangement may be sung in unison through measure 25.

sat - is - fied_____ with Je - sus, sat - is - fied_____ with

Je - sus. Ev - er since that won-der-ful day_____ my

soul's been sat - is - fied._____

Opt. 4th part

My soul is sat - is - fied._____

Talkin' 'bout the Love of God

(S. S. A.)

M. L.

MOSIE LISTER
Arr. by Joseph Linn
S. A. A. arr. by Tom Fettke

Lyrics:
I know a sto-ry, I know it is true;____ And if you lis-ten, I'll tell it to you.____ How some-thing changed me and made me new—

Talk-in' a-bout the love of God._____ A love that gave me a

song to sing,____ And made my win-ters turn in-to spring,____

And gave new mean-ing to ev - 'ry-thing-____

Talk-in' a-bout the love of God.____

Where the Spirit of the Lord Is

(S. S. A.)

R. A.

STEPHEN R. ADAMS
Arr. by Tom Fettke

*two syllables

Spir - it, in the Spir - it of the Lord.

Where the Spir - it of the Lord is,

there is peace; Where the Spir - it of the

Lord is, there is love. There is

com - fort in life's dark - est *hour._ There is light and life; there is
help and pow - er in the Spir - it, in the
Spir - it of the Lord._

*"Welcome, Welcome" (Norris - Reed)
Wel - come, wel - come, wel - come, wel - come!

We're Gonna Make It
(Through the Power of God)
(S. S. A.)

T. and N. B.

JERRY THOMPSON and NILES BOROP
Arr. by Tom Fettke and Randy Smith
S. S. A. arr. by Tom Fettke

With confidence ♩ = ca. 120

CD: 56

We're gon - na make it thro' the pow - er of God, _____ the

pow - er of God, _____ the pow - er of God. _____ Yes,

pow - er that will nev - er fail.

34 *Solo*

Tho' we go thro' fire and flood,____ We're pro - tect - ed by the blood.__ The

blood that Je - sus shed for us____ that day on Cal - va - ry.____ Now

38

De - vil, you can do your best;____ You'll have fail - ure, not suc - cess.__ No

CD: 59

All *f*

mat - ter what your trials or tests,__ We'll win the vic - to - ry. There is

B♭/F   F/A   Gm   Gm⁷   F⁷   B♭

(43) *"There Is Power in the Blood" (Lewis E. Jones)

pow'r,   pow'r,   won - der - work - ing pow'r   In the blood   of the

B♭   B♭⁷   E♭   B♭   F⁷

(47)

Lamb;   There is pow'r,   pow'r,   won - der - work - ing pow'r   In the

B♭   B♭   B♭⁷   E♭   B♭

(51) *Solo*

pre - cious   blood   of the Lamb.   De - vil, you can do your best;

F⁷   F⁹   Dm/F   F⁷   B♭   B♭   B♭/A♭

CD: 60

You'll have fail - ure, not suc - cess. Tho' we go thro' fire and flood,

We're pro - tect - ed by the blood.

We're gon - na make it thro' the pow - er of God, the

pow - er of God, the pow - er of God. Yes,

The Lord Is in This Place

[S. S. A. (A.)]
A cappella

M. L.

MOSIE LISTER
Arr. by Tom Fettke

Pray, broth-ers, pray;———— Pray, sis-ters, pray.————

Pray till the moun-tains melt a - way.————

For Je - sus is near— you, And

Je - sus will hear—you; For sure - ly the

Lord is in this place, in this place.

He Is Here

(S. S. A.)

K. T.

KIRK TALLEY

Arr. by Tom Fettke

name. He is here; you can touch Him. You will

nev - er be_____ the same.

I searched for peace a-mong the shad-ows dark and lone-ly_____ Gave up on find - ing that

The King and I Medley

The King and I
and
Led By the Master's Hand
(S. S. A.)

Arr. by Tom Fettke

*"The King and I (Walk Hand in Hand)" (Mosie Lister)

1st verse: all singing parts
2nd verse: solo or all unison

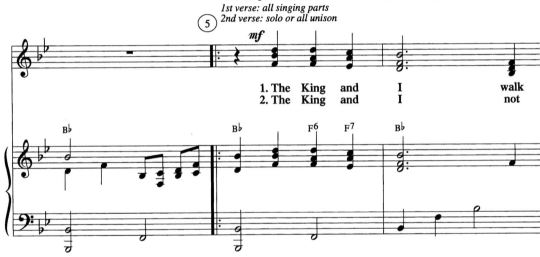

1. The King and I walk
2. The King and I not

down life's road to - geth - er Where man - y
long a - go were stran - gers. I walked a -

*"Led by the Master's Hand" (Mosie Lister)

climb the last_ mile to heav-en's land,_____ I'll be

led by the Mas - ter's hand._____ As I

walk the road of life my feet grow wea - ry,_____

_____ And I stum - ble through the thorns and shift-ing

CD: 70 | 1st time
2nd time to Coda

Solo or all unis

Rise

(S. S. A.)

H. M.

HARLAN MOOR

Arr. by Tom Fett

1. The crip-pled and lame in the road-way_____ Woul
(2.) came with a heart of com-pas-sion,_____ Wit

wait by the hour for the sight Of the sim - ple preach - er fro
love He de-light - ed to heal. ___ The pain of the bro - ken an

Naz-'reth,_____ Who came to set ev - 'ry-thing right. The
lone-ly_____ Was some-thing His spir - it could feel. No

C   A⁷   D

15

pow'r of His touch in an in - stant_____ Could trans-form what tor - ment had
man was too poor for His mer - cy,_____ No man was too rich for His

G   C   G   Em   Em⁷   A⁷

19   CD: 74   2nd time

done;   For He was the Mak-er of heav'n and_ earth,
might;   For He was the Mak-er of heav'n and earth,

B   B⁷   C   G/D   B/D#   Em

2nd time to Coda ⊕   I and II Sop. 𝆑

He was the Al - might - y One.
He was the Ev - er - shin - ing   And He said,

Am⁷   D⁷   D⁷sus   G

"Rise, And He said, "Rise, rise, rise, rise,

rise. Your faith has made you whole a - gain."___ And He said,

gain."___ 2. He

light. 3. To - day we still wait by the road-way;___ We

rise.   Your faith has made you whole   a - gain."_____   And He says,

"Rise,   rise,   rise,   rise,
And He   said, "Rise,

rise.   Your faith has made you whole   a - gain.   A -

rise!"_____

He Knows Just What I Need

(S. S. A.)

M. L.

MOSIE LISTE
Arr. by Tom Fettke and Randy Smi
S. S. A. arr. by Tom Fettk

123

30 a tempo

friends_____ seem to for - get me, When skies are dark,_____ when hope seems

tempo

34

gone, By faith I feel_____ His arms a -

CD: 79

mf *Melody in sop.*

bout me, And hear Him say,_____ "You're not a - lone." My Je- sus

38

cresc.

knows just what I__ need. Oh, yes, He knows just what I___

cresc.

This World Is Not My Home
(S. S. A.)

TRADITIONAL

Arr. by Tom Fettke

melody: sop. II *melody: sop. I*

can't feel at home in this world an-y - more. O

Ab Fm⁷ Bb⁹ Eb⁷ Ab

(63)

Lord, You know I have no friend like You. If

Ab Ab⁷ Db Ab

heav-en's not my home, then Lord, what will I do? The

Ab Fm⁷ Bb⁹ Eb⁷

(67)

an - gels beck - on me from heav- en's o - pen door, And I

Ab Ab⁷ Db Ab

We Shall Rise

[S. S. A. (A.)]
A cappella

L.

MOSIE LISTER
Arr. by Tom Fettke

Reaching

(S. S. A.)

M. L.

MOSIE LISTE
Arr. by Tom Fett

139

I'm Glad I Know Who Jesus Is

(S. S. A.)

G. D.

GERON DAV
Arr. by Tom Fet

(16)

more than just a sto - ry;___ He is the King of Glo - ry. I'm

D   A7/E   D/F#   G

CD: 92

glad   I know who Je - sus is!

D/A   D/F#   G   D/A   A13 A7   D   G

Unison

So___

D/A   D/F#   G   D/A   A13 A7   D   D/C   Bbsus   Ab/Bb

(21)

man - y peo - ple still to-day___ don't know who Je - sus is;   They've

Eb   Ab   Bb7   Eb

nev - er felt His peace with - in their souls. But I

want my life to show them how His love can set them free; He's the

on - ly one who can cleanse and make men whole. I'm

glad I know who Je - sus is! I'm

glad_____ I know who Je - sus is!_____ He's

more than just a sto - ry;____ He is the King of Glo - ry. I'm

2nd time to Coda

Unison

glad I know who Je - sus is! He's t

Al - pha and O - me-ga, the Be - gin-ning and the End; He's